About the Book

Many of our problems in life are because of ignorance of a better way of living. When we become aware of our nature, life, and the correct way of living, our life becomes blissful through correct living. Pain and pleasure both are true. We cannot totally avoid pains in life, but by a proper way of reacting, we can minimize the effects of pain in life. This book, "Verse of wisdom," is all about a better way of living and reacting in our life.

My poems are my feelings, thoughts, and beliefs which I experienced in life. Know Life Through this book I believe you will surely benefit. When you become aware of a wrong living or an attitude in life, there is automatic correction in life. Being a good person not only makes us happy but also brings greater chances of good in our life. Know that we don't become a good person to make others happy, but by being so, it adds value to our life and we become a happy person.

Copyright

All Rights Reserved Worldwide

No part of this publication may be reproduced, stored in or introduced into a retrieval system, or transmitted, in any form, or by any means (electronic, mechanical, photocopying, recording or otherwise), without the prior permission of the Publisher. Any person who commits an unauthorised act in relation to this publication can be liable to criminal prosecution and civil claims for damages.

Disclaimer

This is a work of fiction. The contents of this book are the expressions and opinions of its author and a work of imagination. It does not claim scriptural or historical authenticity. This work does not represent the views of the Publisher nor endorses them in any way. The Publisher makes no representations or warranties as to the completeness or accuracy of the information used.

Table of Content

- **Detachment** — 01
- **Selfless Love** — 13
- **Voice of Wisdom** — 23
- **About Life** — 41
- **An Attitude** — 50
- **Love** — 80

Table of Content

- **Detachment**   01
- **Selfless Love**   13
- **Voice of Wisdom**   23
- **About Life**   41
- **An Attitude**   50
- **Love**   80

Chapter 1
Detachment

Know that pleasure and displeasure both are short lived. When we meet a pleasure it fascinates us and a desire takes birth. When more and more we think about this desire the more we get attached to it. This attachment increases our expectations. But the pleasure of this desire being shorter than our expectations leads us to disappointment and misery. It is like two people fighting to come in to your life. One is pleasure and the other is displeasure. You have to solve this fight. When you get emotionally attached with both you go through misery because when pleasure says I am right you agree to it and feel nice and when displeasure says I am right you believe it. The reason being ignorance because they both are short lived and are not your true nature. When you step aside and solve this fight without getting emotionally attached then in that case you don't go through misery since now you know both are right for a moment only. This wisdom and your detachment brings joy in life.

Distance Living

Everybody is lone
Living in fantasy
Seeking something to carry on
To fill up space empty

No wonder their dream shatter
And they mourn
For they are lone traveller
Which they don't own

Happy are they who detach
From every thing
Love self and others but don't attach
And believe in distance living.

03

Renounce the world

When the world hurts it pains-

so much so

The heart sinks ,

The limbs numb remains

And the Heart restless in the go

No place comforts

No one sooths

The mind torments

And the soul slowly broods

Ask my heart -

What is that called wrong?

It will tell -to hurt

The only law amidst all among

And what is truth?

It will tell there is no law

In the affairs of life and death

And this is God's creation i saw

And what is the truth that the sage seek?

It will tell it is eternal bliss

Which is none but peace in a soul meek

That comes after detachment from world this

To be selfless

Without climbing mountain
Can't reach the top
Peace you attain
When you reach up

Like a sun rise
Let there be light
A soul that is wise
Can only conquer height

A tree that bears fruit
Can only give
For there is joy in it
In giving what you have

Toil, rise, and shed to be selfless
Joy you will own
Since you are carrying less
And less on you is the burden

Life an energy

What is this life?

Is it endlessly to produce and spread grief ?

Is it a fight for a piece of land?

Is it material wealth in hand?

Is it to dominate?

Is it to hate?

It is none of these

It is simply peace

Which comes when you understand

And with it comes joy in mind

so understand life

Amidst your problems rife

Amidst your pleasure and pain

Amidst your efforts in vain

It is just an energy

Which makes you happy

So detach yourself from all that, which it is not

Otherwise to feel this life you cannot.

Dreams that shatter

Don't run after fantasy

you will fail to live the present,

and will be unhappy

life is just an energy;

which makes you feel good,

when you have no wants and don't run after any.

in this life's journey

walk with love,

it will make you happy.

 you will have this love

when you are at peace,

with yourself; and around the world you have.

 Remember if you want peace

you have to avoid all that troubles,

otherwise you won't ease.

Remember you will overcome troubles and will be free

when you accept this imperfect world and learn to live

and don't run after fantasy.

And where will you find how to Live

It's in your awareness,

of all the wisdom you have.

Rise above good and evil

There will be always a battle
Between the good and the evil
Both in their own way an extremist
Who fight to exist

Selfish in their own way
Since they fight come what may
One for righteousness
Other for unrighteousness

And what is right?
Is it to be selfish and fight?
Or is it a soul's battle
To rise above good and evil ?

That which is ours
will eventually come back to us
All the battles
Had their evils

Those who won
were not happy it's known

Know there is a way
Of kindness and giving away

Can a man have more than his fate?
He is not destined for that
One who is kind all the while
He only rises above good and evil.

Life in universe is eternal

My heart why are you so sad
I think thoughts of death is troubling you
what is there to feel bad ?
Life is a bundle of awareness to go through

Don't get attached to the memories
just feel life's varied colours
And the joy is in continuance of these
which a reincarnated life assures

why you want to carry memories
You have to leave it
Then only your new life the Joy of fresh awareness it
carries
don't feel sad, in this universe life will continue to exist.

Joy of Detachment

Today I met death
I was in search of life
A feeling of such a depth
Which put off problems rife

It made me to detach
From all the affairs
Making a joy hatch
Which my heart airs

I saw life from a distance
There was peace
Not much involved hence
Which made me ease

Oh! I wonder, it brought what wealth?
For I was meeting life with death
Living in the middle of both
It was such a sheer joyous wealth.

Detachment

What is it to detach?--

Is it not to love?,

Surely not;

But to love selflessly and with trust catch

Otherwise to avoid insecure feelings you cannot.

Is it not to do your duty?--

Surely not;

Since that will not set you free

And to feel joy you cannot.

Is it to stop living?--

Surely not;

But to remain less involving

Without which at peace you cannot.

To detach means --

To cut all the ties,

That in life negatively remains,

And affecting our freedom lies.

Peace satisfies

Let me cut the ties

Of all that lies

In the way of my peace

For it satisfies

Didn't the desire disappoint

Being greedy was the point

Didn't the life put me down

When more I wanted to own

My heart nothing satiates

Except my peaceful States

So let me detach

From all that I attach

Let me ever carry this thought

That i am happy with what I got

Oh I feel nice

For being wise

Oh I feel nice

For being wise.

Chapter 2
Selfless Love

"Selfless Love" is a chapter consisting poems expressing author's opinion about love. Love is different from fascination and possession. A true love is selfless. Like the love of a mother for her child. The child never doubts the love of the mother. Then why is this not the case with the rest of the world. It is because we are selfish in our love of the world. Which leads to possession and then misery. Somebody has rightly said that if you love someone set them free if they come back they are yours and if they don't they never was. There is no joy in possession. One more thing that troubles us is that we want perfection in a relationship. We have to keep room for other's imperfections. Nobody is perfect all the time.

14

Love is eternal

My eyes tear

Heart laments for you

For the fate separates us dear

Should the love die too?

Can the spring fail,

To make the flowers bloom?

Then how can life, make my love nil;

And put to doom?

Love is ever there

Before our birth

In the time we are

And will be after our death

The universe, can never be without an ocean

Nor it can be without a star to shine

So do my affection

And the urge to make you mine.

15

Love never harms

Can a Rose harm?

Or fali to attract?

Or can it fali to make the heart warm ?

It is your act-

That wants to possess

With lack of love

Hurt in the process

That a piercing thorn gave

A heart full of love

Can never hate

It's sheer joy to have

Capable to sate

Attachment is misery

It is bondage

It will not set you free

A thing not of sage

Love matters

Take a pause when there is rush
Whether in life or inside you
Must not you miss the streams of love i wish
That flows for dear ones in you

Time once lost will never come back
with it those who loved, and reared you
At the end of life, what time you lack
what will matter is cherished memories of loving you

Nothing in life fills you more
Than the love life of you
In place of this whatever gained know for sure
Will make life empty for you.

17

Deep Love

A love's gentle smile
Makes the heart melt
And soothes it for a while
Is there any words dealt?

And the longing eyes
For a moment met
To convey love suffice
Is there any words dealt?

The Hearts in oneness
And all that felt
Is often in stillness
There is no word dealt.

what is there in words ?
It's empty without emotions
The calm of the woods
The depth of the oceans
Are to be felt.

Selfless love

It was very tall

For to measure

pure blind love i should call

that made my eyes profoundly tear

A love of deer for its fawn

should i call it a sacrifice

Word too short to dawn

I saw it with my eyes

Both were grazing by the stream

In a short while

To cross the Fawn started to swim

And was chased by a crocodile

seeing the danger the mother swam in between

Until the Fawn crossed stood there

The crocodile caught and took away the mother in scene

And nothing could stop my eyes tear.

Distress masks love

In deep river

the current is more

one knows not

who is standing at the shore

The beauty of flower

attracts the calm heart more

one knows not

who's heart is sore

so is love's nature

Like a beautiful flower and deep river

one knows not

When in trouble with their lover

Love never dies

I know it's easy to say , "I love you"

But not that easy , To be that way

All life through , When I said

I was true

Sometimes I couldn't feel

In our hard times , That turned us blue

I even thought of going far away

Leaving you

But beloved

I could not walk away

Steps one or two , Such is our love

Without it , We cannot do

Today is our twenty seventh

Marriage anniversary

And a day to cherish our memories

And Our love too

I want you to be happy

An ideal life seldom exists

Know it's true

What matters the most is--

I still love you.

Nature of love

Like a soothing wind
That calms the mind
Like a beautiful flower
That attracts the viewer
Like a soaring eagle
That flies over a hill
Like a chirping Bird
That sings without a word
Like a Clement weather
That Joys the dweller
So is love's nature
That dwells in a feeling heart's core

Accept imperfection

Nothing is permanent
but we run after perfection
without contentment
be it attitude, behaviour, or love in relation
we want the ideal
Which is why we are constantly in conflict
because we are seeking the unreal
when a man takes the other as he is
with a room for his imperfection
than that is wise
And only then there will be compassion
which is heavenly
we can make this earth an heaven
not by perfect rules many
but by accepting imperfection.

Chapter 3
Voice of Wisdom

"Voice of Wisdom" is a collection of poems that showcase the author's wisdom gained from various life experiences. Venkateshan shares his insights on topics such as human nature, relationships, and spirituality, inviting readers to contemplate their own beliefs and values. Through his poems, he encourages readers to think critically and to look beyond surface-level appearances to find deeper truths. The poems in this chapter are reflective and thought-provoking, offering readers a glimpse into the author's unique perspective on life.

Illusion

This world is an illusion
Since it fascinates at the first vision;
Then, finally fails to satiate;
When we achieve it.
So it's a painful affair,
To indulge in desire;
For, a desire will disappoint,
Soon after you realize it.
It will trouble you in one more way;
From a blissful self, it will carry you astray;
By making you lose, the awareness;
Of your dutiful affairs.
There is no greater bliss, that a man acquires,
Than this self awareness.

God is within me

No religion is greater

Than, benevolence and harmlessness

I abide to thus ever

For, they are God's act of selflessness

God is in my nature and deed

Always from within to guide

When he approves, what I do is right

I doesn't matter; even if I fit wrong, in world's sight

In moments; with God, when not in oneness

To him, and to the wronged; I ask for forgiveness

From God's path when my path sways

A call to me he gives always

Be on the side of just

Be ever kind

But carry this in your mind

while solving a grievance

Be involved your loved ones

Always be on the side of right

No matter how hard on your heart it might

Seeing your loved ones stand unjust

Supporting them please don't rest

If you do, that will spoil your loved ones

And seldom it will solve the grievance

Love and justice are two different things

Steady in both makes us lovely beings

When everyone takes the unjust way

Broken into groups the society will lay

There will be conflicts

Which ever afflicts.

God you must prevail

God you must prevail

To show the righteous path

When astray and wickedness our nature hath

To lead to peaceful life

When restlessness dwells in our mind and is rife

To save us from sin

When evil deludes us and tries to win

To lead to blissful living

When ignorance blocks our blissful path of being

To protect us from destruction

When enmity creates a warlike condition

To make goodness prevail in world

When evil tries to get hold

God you must prevail

God you must prevail

God I want to travel light

God I want to travel light

When I lie, or ill-intention I have

with anxiety I will live

Hatred for others, in me when I nurture

Hostile feelings towards them I will gather

Enemies when I gather

Will lose peace of mind forever

Towards other when I grow anger

Will cause suffering to self and other

To someone when I am cruel

Its an unjust act I feel

So moral rules when I foul

It's a burden to my soul

God, I want to travel light

God, I want to travel light

Don't get even

Someone when breaks thy heart;

Don't persuade them to love,

Nor should thee hurt;

Or should they break thy trust;

Don't lose mind,

Forgive, relax and rest;

Should not thee give hurt for a hurt;

Thy heaven will fall apart;

Suspicion when clouds thy way,

With trust, in righteous path thee must stay;

Because, the right way goes to heaven,

when thee don't get even;

The other way goes to hell,

When thy negative emotions unable to quell.

God give me Strength

In life, when there is trouble

And the road I walk is all uphill

Someone when ill-treats me

And pain, in my heart to be

Someone when deceives

And world in such, when my heart believes

Someone when wounds

And pain crosses all bounds

God give me strength- so that, calm I become

And that, with patience, my ill fate, I overcome

For, to overcome a situation given

When with patience, it quickly restores my lost heaven

Whenever my negative emotion I found unable to quell

Eventually, for long,I ended up in hell

31
A wise way

In the life's affair

If you find; someone, not fair

On a dispute, losing their mind

Dear,towards them; remain calm and kind

Its futile, to condemn them I say

Or to argue , or to indulge in fray

Rules of conduct,when they violate

Its wise to tolerate

Uplift them with patience

By removing their ignorance

For a good soul

Deserves a gentle cleanse when foul

And an evil one

Will never listen; are ill-fated , should be left alone

Sometimes, in someway, we all are not perfect

And to be ever perfect, its unwise to expect

On being perfect

In order to conquer the sky
Have to learn how to fly
To enjoy the food
It has to be cooked deliciously good
A lion's cub, learns the surviving skill
When it learns from mother, how to kill
Similarly, to make life ever joyous
Have to learn, to be virtuous
To be virtuous, don't have to be flawless
But, have to aim, to be harmless
When happen to hurt, just have to say sorry
Then in life, don't have to worry
Only these rules together when we hold
It will take care of the virtuous world

33

Faith

A fisherman fishing in a lake

Knew that the lake had a poisonous snake

In his boat, he also took people on ferry

Who, just came there for time merry

He used to caution people about the danger

That-"there is a snake underwater

In water, don't put in your hand

Please carry this in your mind"

Those believed him; refrained

Others lacking faith did not entertained

and played with their life

Since, under water there was danger rife

Sometimes;a danger, a misery; we can't see

To have faith in word of caution is wise to be

For we will be benefited

And those who lack faith may be ill-fated

What good is that joyous path

That in it's way miseries hath

Having faith is like God

It protects us from miseries, danger in times odd

Blissful paths

A life, which is a social one
Is better than a life, which is lone
A know how of work
Will ease our troubles and not make us a jerk
A troubles foresight
Will prevent in ending in a plight
A desire which was with a detachment
When unfulfilled, will be of less disappointment
A way full of patience
Is less troubling than a way of rude and arrogance
All such wisdom filled paths will give much peace
Life will be one of ease
And will be one that constantly joy gains
Since life was, a series of avoidance of pains

Surrender

There is much pain

In the journey of gain

While we seek

And while we try to achieve the peak

To the fate surrender

For a way better

Not like the one who stops striving

Not like the one who stops living

But like the one who is above all dual states

Who neither desires nor hates

Who sees joy and sufferings of others as their own

To whom a precious gem and a clod of earth is one

Who chooses the path of wisdom

Ever to guide them

In the times of honours, dishonours, pleasures, and pains;

Ever serene who remains.

Who's actions selfless

Such a life will be filled with more of bliss.

Freedom

When I can't see

My future, how its going to be

When fears creeps in to my mind

And my heart longs for a helping hand

In all of my doubts

And in my moments of desperate bouts

Let me have faith in God

That his every plan is to bring out in me good

Now when darkness on my ways lays

Let me willingly accept these days

Let me ever for life keep striving

Let me keep going

Understanding his plans for me, with patience and

faith

Even if one leads me to death

It is his plan, let me be ever happy

In whatever courses, he sets me

This is the only way to freedom

For this way, to my fears, there will be no room.

A wind's play

It's a stormy night
My room lit by an oil lamp's light
The rushing wind from the window
Plays with the lamp's glow
This affair between lamp's glow and wind
Evokes a thought in my mind
The oil lamp represents me
And the wind the circumstances to be
When the wind is rough and strong
The lamp's glow flickers all along
And when the wind is gentle
It glows ample
When the wind is still
It glows steady and it is peaceful
Unless quelled by a squall
The lamp will glow till it consumes oil all.

You make me rise

When I look at you I rise; don't know why
Probably; God your place in my heart is high
I shed away my dirt
And pure becomes this heart
My inner anxious calls becomes silent
All my problems seems less salient
I feel calm and light
Everything falls in its place and seems right
That its futile to fight;
I rise to such a height
To let go is right I realise
And I rise, rise, and rise.

God

He lives in the heart and mind,

An ideal being called God,

To be ever Kind

Towards those who are good,

Ever forgiving and guiding.

When his people commit sin,

He is an ever loving and never hurting being,

Who makes his people happily grin

Such is his ideal image

To imbibe in our hearts

And to live his way throughout our age,

Otherwise this life hurts.

He protects his people

From those who don't believe in his ways.

For they are evil

Who will harm his people always.

He works through his people's hands.

For he is within us

In our deeds, hearts, and minds

To make this world blissful thus.

There is also a creator

Who created life of various forms,

...

Equally good.
Not interfering in our life and
Transcendental in nature,
Who is called the supreme God.

Humanity

Worship any God,
It won't be of any good;
Follow any religion,
It's purpose becomes an oblivion;
Go to any shrine,
A futile thing it will remain;
When they can't make you towards people-
Kind, forgiving, loving and gentle.

Chapter 4
About Life

"About Life" contains poems that examine different facets of life. Through his writing, Venkateshan explores the complexities of human existence, from the joyous moments to the more challenging times. He encourages readers to embrace life's many twists and turns, to find beauty in unexpected places, and to appreciate the fleeting nature of time. The poems in this chapter are evocative and inspiring, encouraging readers to make the most of every moment.

God's purpose for us

He created all of his creations with an aim

The supreme god we call him

Each of his creations, his assigned purpose attains

Their simple living itself achieves his purpose, and his world sustains

By giving desire and pleasure to us

He achieves continuance of his creations thus

With pleasure he also made pain

Thus breaking the monotonous pleasure to seek it again

Gave us intellect to seek that which is best

For he wanted survival of the fittest

We as humans go a step further and wonder his creations

Some don't believe in him out of ignorance

Some study his creations and see its essence

That all have been created from seed,

This confirms his presence

Only some higher spirits get closer to him knowing this

With a vain attempt to see who he is

I wonder in this pensive moment,

Did he created this world for his entertainment?

43

A scene

I was in my deep sleep

God wakes me up to a scene

Called life, where I smile, cry, laugh, and weep

Love, hate, joy, and sorrow, having seen

First I thought I can change what's going on

Then realised only the way I react

For he is the only one

The master of act

So what if more of trouble I see

Giving me much pain

I am only the spectator to be

Who is destined to a deep sleep again

Puppet

When things go as per our wish

In life's run and rush

We feel we are master of our destiny

That there is no role of fate or any

But it's a myth

For our plan with fate was one with

When things go wrong

And we struggle for long

We feel very weak

And before fate meek

For we were on wrong path

Something different our fate hath

Whether as per our wish or not

Everything our fate has brought

We only realise it very late

That we are puppets in the hands of fate

45
Life

Life, has a different meaning at different stages

Its wrong to perceive life by one name;

But, the old taught such to young from ages;

that, it's a renouncing theme

A child, would seldom think of death

He is full of excitement

God gears up a child for youth

For a desire he is meant

To be involved in it

To give birth to a new offspring

To make life continue to exist

This is God's planning

As a child, we understand life as a desire

Until, this desire ends up in disappointment

In adult age, after appeasing our hunger

Here, life in a suffering, and we long detachment.

In old age, in God's world

To get liberated from suffering is our aspiration

For god doesn't wants us to desire hold

Thus we see here; life, as a Liberation

Knowing this, always try to be happy

In life, sufferings and sorrow will come

Still see, life as a joyous journey

Take everything light, life blissful will become

Only a freedom fighter feels real joy of freedom

Purpose of life

To delight, a purpose of the flower

Through it's nectar, fragrance, and beauty forever

In analogy, nectar represents in us a sweet nature

Fragrance, the capacity to create good atmosphere

And the beauty ,

an attractive personality

Such being, some from a distance admire

Some to possess acquire

And some love

For they are great pleasure in life to have

whether flower is offered to God in a temple

Or forms part of decoration in home of people

Be it wherever, it only spreads happiness

So is the purpose of our life similar to it

For to spread happiness and one day to quit

In life, to experience and witness

The life's varied colours

Like simple calm dwellers

Whatever memories up gathered with

Everything to end with death

Life a joyous journey

A thought made me to bother

What does this life really mean ?

Is it blissful ever ?

With eternal joy in a life's scene

Sense pleasures do elate

But has a short fate

Having work and purpose

Doesn't solve moments of distress

Then came to me a philosophy

To see death as the destination

And life a joyous journey

Where comes each and every in between station

Some are joyless

And some a bliss

While all memories are built

Both of joy and sorrow to lit.

Life a dream

Neither I was before my birth

Nor I will be after my death

This in between time to live

Is like a wonderful dream I believe

Bounded either side by tenebrosity

This dream exist between two harsh reality

Love, peace and joy, to be seen

In a serene scene

Not to be spoiled by fights and bitterness

Filled with move of happiness

It is brief either

It's waste of time fighting and being bitter

After death nothing matters, be it any lived deed

But when alive deeds matter, one of my creed

For I wish to see a ravishing dream

Not a nightmare to scream

49

Duality of life

A rising sun has to set

So do our happiness lasts for a moment

In life, whenever joy and sorrow we get

Both passes away, with time spent

Sometimes we feel happy and sometimes sad

In life to attain a state of eternal bliss;

An ideal thought, which makes us glad

But nothing lasts forever, a truth this is

In a year, spring season comes

So do fall

Thus is life, duality, a reality it becomes

And this a nature's truth we call

Pleasure and pain both are true

When wounded we can choose to be calm

And even decide not to react too

But false if we say, the wound didn't harm

Chapter 5
<u>An Attitude</u>

"An attitude" offers poems that provide practical advice and guidance for those struggling with pain and suffering. Venkateshan draws on his own experiences and observations to offer insights on topics such as resilience, perseverance, and hope. The poems in this chapter are empowering and encouraging, reminding readers that they have the strength and ability to overcome even the most challenging of circumstances.

Change in the wind

I believe there is change in the wind

My life was troubled

Disappointments hailed storming the mind

And my tears dribbled

My heart filled with gloom

Amid loved ones, led a life of solitude

Then, with no fear of doom

Adopts a renouncing attitude

Worldly pleasures are like morning twilight

They last for a period brief

Where as renouncing them is like daylight

Brings long lasting peace and joy to life

It doesn't mean I will stop living

But instead live with detachment

Remain in this world striving

To live life and meet my every commitment

I will rest my happiness on what I have

Than on things, for the movement which are impossible

Making my affordable world likeable to live

Thus leading a life which is sensible

Never Give up

When the sea is rough

And your sailing becomes tough

In the darkest hours of the night

Should the shore seem out of sight

Worries when takes away your rest and sleep

In your heart when fears creep

When there is loss of hope

And you find difficult to cope

It's time to gather strength to fight

To strive to come out of your plight

Against all odds to take every winning step

But never should you give up

Be independent

This heart learnt a lesson
That never depend for living
For none own
A mother's heart in giving

It will cost self-esteem one day
And nothing you will own
There will be no joy
And you will mourn

A gift has little worth
For it has come free
No matter how great in wealth
It will fail to make you happy

What joy is in begging?
No matter what little you earn
Remember you will be a king
Since that you own.

Socialize

It was like finding an oasis in a desert

To my thirst

Like a spring that brings blossom

It made my love bloom

Deeper than the ocean

Was the affection

Calmer than the Wood

Was the mood

Like chirping of birds

Soothed the words

Such was my reunion with kith and kin

Which made me joyfully grin

Making memories to cherish

It was such a fulfilled wish

What a bliss!

What a bliss!

Preserve peace of mind

Peace of mind is like a rose flower

In order to have it

Should know, to avoid thorns, in plant all over

Thorns means wrong paths, negative emotions thee must quit

When a difficult situation sweeps,

To a wrong path or to a negative emotion

Withdraw saying sorry, even walked a few steps

Much pain will be avoided, by stopping the motion

Be like a tall grass

Swaying in a storm it survives

Where as a rigid tree, big in mass;

Gets uprooted, for it resists the storm that destroys.

Preserve peace of mind

Until it gets lost, thee won't realise its worth

In life unperturbed happiness thee will find

Only when peace thy mind hath

56

Diary

The mind has a diary

To write into it known as memory

Got two pens to write

One in black and the other in white

All in life that is bright

You write with a pen that is white

Moments when you are bitter

Then with black pen you are a writer

Here others too write

And so do the fate

But be careful what you write

In all case try to make it in white

What you write matters the most

Has such a power to turn better from worst

When it happens to be in black

To make you happy it will lack

When you recollect your life

The bitter part will hurt you like knife

So be careful with your life known what

You can make it dull or bright

Not to this it will stop

Will effect your future when happiness you shop

The diary has also pages in red

To write on it you must dread

Red symbolises an aggressive emotion

On which emotions to write should choose with caution

Our World

Our world is no different than a jungle

In animal world, the law is survival of the fittest

Our's need a flawless image to freely mingle

Because if we breach its norms, it will protest

It won't consider the reason or the truth

Will crucify us even if we are a saint

And in some cases it can cause even death

So why give our world chance to point

Cases of honour killing

Opposed by world lovers ending their love affair

Are all because in our day to day living;

To our world, tolerance and mercy doesn't seems fair

So right or wrong, it's sad to stand alone

We need our world, a fact final

Be with it and change it to a better one

Because man is a social animal

Self Worth

Success in order to get

Should have capabilities to achieve it

To stay in high position

Need to have qualities to handle people and vision

Desire beautiful spouse for thee

Only on a similar ground when thee are worthy

Have only that much money

Which able to guard, to thy life not an enemy

Because success, positon, beautiful spouse, and wealth

At all times demand thy worth

When thee not worthy and have them

Results in failure to maintain, and sometimes fatal they

become

Thee may need a help

Be generous towards other

Someday thee might need a favour

Forgive others mistake

Thee when wrong might want them to forsake

Help the needy even it is out of the way

Thee may need a help, as good times always don't stay

Sympathize with those who suffer a loss

May need sympathy while misfortune thee cross

Give company to the lone

So that someday thee are not left alone

Unwise is he who thinks he can do himself

Mostly to such life loneliness and gloom will engulf

The power of forgiveness

My conscious mind pure

Like a crystal clear water

Which the world dirts one day

That blurred my vision and took me astray

Failed to see what was wrong

For a moment carried along

Now the serpent of quilt

Got wound around me to hit

I woke up suddenly

And struggled to set myself free

For freedom I yearned

From mistake I learned

But the serpent didn't gave up

It increased its grip

For help I cried

The one whom I wronged came to my side

I said please forgive and help

Before the serpent could kill me and gulp

And he forgave and helped in my dismay

Rescued me, and took the serpent away

I wondered when someone concerned forgives

How our distress it relieves

For they are the right ones

Who can help at once

Such is the power of forgiveness

It restores our peace and happiness

Happy life

Like a thirsty deer which runs after a mirage

Behind happiness we run throughout our age

Being thus we never achieve it

For we believe it, as something eternal and complete

There is no worldly pleasure

That once experienced will elate forever

A musk deer searches outside its own scent

Similarly we search happiness outside ,but lies within to
hunt

Happiness comes- when we-expect less and find more

Love ourselves and others to the core

Search inward, find, achieve, those that makes us glad

Find solution for those that makes us sad

Know some solutions lies with wisdom and science

And some when we renounce

Learn this life has not much to offer

And in life have meaningful purpose ever

A choice

One day I have to die

Nothing can avert this, no matter how much I cry

The choice is mine

Whether to choose darkness or sunshine

Love or hate

Fight or a peaceful state

Wisdom or ignorance

Anger or patience

The negative choices in life will make problems rife

The positive choices will give a sweet life

The problems will make seem life hard and long for me

A sweet life, will make, short and sweet my journey

Victim of circumstances

The mind is restless
Not fully disturbed but a bit less
For its peaceful and joyous state,
the present state of affairs do frustrate
Everything is against it
And there is no way to quit
It longs to set itself free
And wants to live life fully
No matter how calm in present state of affairs
It loses joy and peace, and sadness it airs
When situation unpleasant to our senses
We become victim of circumstances

I will always try to be happy

When I get less

I will give more and find bliss

When unfulfilled my desire

I will dream it again and feel higher

When disappointed in love

I will love myself and live

When there is loneliness

I will enjoy the calmness

When I am unhappy

I will enjoy the sadness to be

When my path is thorny

I will enjoy the agony

When there is nothing for celebration

I will try to find compersion

When fate gives me the worst

I will try to make it my best

Whatever fate handovers me

I will always try to be happy

65
Paths Of Life

One path is to be worldly

Striving and earning our living

Here we desire desperately

In this path of being worldly in desiring

When fulfilled feel happy and when not leads to

depression

To feel thus attachment to fruits of desire is the reason

Still we believe the path worth trudging

For the things desired are worth realising

The other path is to remain saintly

Which comes after desires renouncing

A life which is very much plainly

And of subtle eternal happiness in leading

Nothing to disappoint makes us a calm being

To remain in this world watching

The worlds varied colours

Like simple silent dwellers

I suggest, remain worldly but saintly willed

That is seeking a thing desired with detachment

Which gives happiness when fulfilled

And we remain unaffected by disappointment

For there is no attachment to fruit of desire

So it doesn't pains when the desire ends up in failure

A painless middle path

Always in life to walk with

To be the way are flowers

This life many things it offers

For we are born with many desires

But one way to be the way are flowers

When life much sorrow it bears

The flower's fragrance and beauty to attract the bees

And its nectar, them to satiate

To carry its pollen to other flowering trees

Thus flowers seeks joy, and we in our mate

When our life similar to life of that flower

which was plucked

Somewhere to offer

With all its paths to joy blocked

Be like it, that still lavished its beauty

And fragrance in life all the while

To love our new world, and do our duty

Always with a smile

Who never lets down

God when I was young

I didn't realised your worth then

With many others you lived among

As someone who is ever silent and in heaven

Childhood passed with parents

youth with spouse and children

Then came old age and those moments

When the world made me sullen

Everyone to let me down at some point

It's not that they don't care

But there was moments that did disappoint

My soul searched someone who will be always there

It was then I turned towards you

As someone who is ever present

Who never lets down and always listens to

some one to whom all my emotions I can vent

Hence I started visiting temple

To a heavenly state which hauls

Where I found peace of mind ample

And also company of alike souls

Calms me this ringing bell

Calm's me this ringing bell

Prayer at temple in hill

I find myself in other world

Far away from world wild

To supreme god I surrender

Dissolving my ego under

In tranquillity of his temple

I find peace of mind ample

I unload my every burden

A faith will dissolve my burdens even

With him I discuss my every problem

In peace I find solution for them

For he is my only hope

He even gives me strength to cope

And I gather from him will

To accomplish all things well

I visit him often

For divine becomes this human

He has such a power

To turn righteous even a greatest sinner

Life a commitment

Neither see life, ever a bed of Roses

Nor see it that, that ever stresses

Neither see it ever lucrative

Nor see it ever destructive

Neither see it ever yielding to desires

Nor see it ever filled with despairs

Neither see it ever as per wishes

Nor see it ever filled with disrelishes

Neither see it ever an enjoyment

Nor see it ever a torment

See it as commitment for always

To make the best of that, which it lays

Change is life

Life is like a scenic journey

While going through this scenery

Life will be; bubbling on seeing a babbling river

Attractive at the sight of a beautiful nature

Difficult while climbing a big mountain

Gloomy under clouds that darkness maintain

Bright in a day light

Unlit in a dark Night

Whatever be the case

With life we have to keep pace

We can stop at none

Until we reach our destination

Because if we stop in between and till end wait

Life after sometime will fail to elate

For change is life

And to stop is like death rife

Smile

Remember to smile

All the while

Be it joy

Or troubles high

When you are happy

Or sad to be

In times of stress

Or of stillness

In moments of success

Or of loss

When fate is pulling down

Do not frown

Whomever you meet

With a smile greet

Be a spectator feeling light

In your day and night

Remember to smile

All the while

Remember to smile

All the while

Prayer song

It's going to be alright

I will be out of this plight

It's a passing phase

Everything is going to ease

Let me have patience

It's a least pain hence

If I hurt feeling quarry

I will say sorry

It's going to be alright

I will be out of this plight

It's a passing phase

Everything is going to ease

Let me cleanse my heart

of all accumulated dirt

It will reduce my burdens

When normal life begins

It's going to be alright

I will be out of this plight

It's a passing phase

Everything is going to ease

It's going to be alright

It's going to be alright

Thee find a song

Thee find a song

of deep thought similar to thy present emotion

To listen, hum, and sing

At time romantic, troubled, or solitude one

Sing till thee vent thy emotion

To fill thy heart with peace

An emotion be it of love or of frustration

A song in such time will ease

In them thee will find oneness with thy feeling

And will be in a fantasy world

Which in sympathetic and soothing

Whenever thee find thy life cold

Fond memories

A thing to do with loved ones before I die

Have to create fond memories before i say goodbye

In this remaining time to spend

With fond memories I want to end

Will heal the wounds to any that I gave

Not bitter memories but only fond ones to have

Forever in their memories to cherish

Even after from this world when I perish

75

A Gift

Daughter today on your twenty second birthday

I Thought what gift to give you this day

Gold ornaments? Diamonds? But they can be lost

Then I decided something that will ever last

In life some we love and choose

And we never want them to lose

But by fate some come to live with us

And with them we may not feel oneness

It takes efforts to get along well with all

Small efforts with some and with some efforts tall

To all always remain nice

Know that this way is wise

Take everything in a light way

Many times people don't mean to hurt by what they say

Be close to near and dear

those dislike you, from a distance them bear

know that you have to carry every one

If you start deleting you will be left alone

lift yourself to a high place

where, those dislike you with patience them you face

For they are ignorant of a better living

If possible try to win them by way loving,

and by remaining calm;

Ever forgiving them even if they harm

If you happen to lose patience;

with a word of sorry resolve at once.

sometimes we have to go through small pains;

so that life has some of the big gains.

An ideal relationship seldom exist;

to run after it you must resist.

Please accept my gift these words of wisdom;

To face the world it will groom.

77

An Attitude

When things don't work out my way

And the path I walk thorny lay

Over these troubles

Let me move, like a cloud moves over hills

Without getting much involved there

Let me not averse them, nor over care

In life, coexists both ease and trouble

And in world, coexists both Good and evil

This will be there always

Life sometimes will be unfair in many ways

Like a cloud, let me float over them

Otherwise, to me much painful they will become

Let I be happy for all that is Good

And be ever grateful to God

78

Payback

My every cell of body belongs to her

She is mother of all, the mother nature

Ever she attracts me

With her unique beauty

Be it food

Or clothes to look good

Everything she offers

For a kind heart She bears

My heart, ever a joyous child in her lap

But a regret, that her health we do sap

I feel to her I am ever in debt

And nothing will be move apt

than to return her favour

By a deed forever

When I die, bury me bare under mother Earth

Let my body nourish her after death

Over this place plant a tree

For flora fed me all life free

I don't wish to be turned into ashes

This is one of my last wishes

One another wish I hold

Its a desire to payback to the world

79

Let know my poems to every child

I hope he will not make this world wild

You will find these poems in my place

I have kept them safe in a suitcase.

Chapter 6
Love

"Love" is a collection of poems that explore the many dimensions of love. Venkateshan writes about the highs and lows of romantic relationships, as well as the love that exists between family members and friends. The poems in this chapter are tender and heartfelt, expressing the author's deep appreciation for the people in his life. Through his writing, Venkateshan reminds readers of the transformative power of love and the importance of cultivating meaningful connections with others.

81
Soul Mates

We only met yesterday
When our eyes met on the way
A powerful attraction towards you
Which is very sweet to bear too
Our hearts beats in oneness
Let me tell you it is such a bliss
My heart bears a sweet pain
To meet you and spend time again
With some we live for years
Still a distance the hearts bears
No matter how many good wills we gather
The hearts never comes together
In life among all those who we meet
Only some we like and are sweet
For they take us to many blissful states
And are called our soul mates

You are my life

You in my mind
Since I was a boy
For to be kind
In the moments of joy
searched you in each face
In nobody I could find a trace
Sometimes desperate to find you
Life seemed meaningless too
In my moments of despair
Its you that I longed
Somebody who could care
in moments when I am wronged
Without you all festivals lifeless
All occasions less pompous
Until I found you
I just stopped living too
One day found you to have
my joy had no bound
This heart found one to love
Someone who is jocund
Having you my world seems beautiful
My life meaningful and purposeful
As I found you
I became lively too

What I love

It's not your curly dense hair

Neither your slim figure

Nor your beautiful eyes

Beloved that ties

It's the unconditional way you love

The harmless way you behave

The oneness that you show

And your innocence that never to go

It's the selfless way you care

And the sincere way you are

I love the nature in you

to you that bonds me it's true

Without you

Without you this world hurts

To express there is short of words

My love, no place comforts

Not even pleasures leading roads

Bright lights hurts my eyes

I seek places of dim lights

At heart loneliness lives

In awake and pensive nights

I run away from crowd

I long for you to be;

In my solitude;

For; to comfort and accompany.

So much I love you

An incident from our young wed days

How much I love you it conveys

You were leaving to your mother's place

Before you left I remember we did embrace

That day when I sat alone

long after you have gone

a Long hair, in my sleeve, caught my attention

It put me in a difficult situation

It was your hair

And nothing could stop my tear

I was terribly missing you

Time was difficult to pass through

Mind said stop, part, its just a hair

Heart said no, its of my love, I care

I could not part with it

And I carefully placed it in my pocket

It soothed and gave me company

Until you came back to me

So much i love you

Everything of you I treasure its True.

Love

Want to share my feelings for thee

It's thee that I ever long

In life to live and share pleasures among

Very much fond of thee

Without thee can't think of me

Thee, never I want to possess

Instead want a willing free spirit which all pains eases

Whenever thy company I found

My joy had no bound

Without thee, my world falls apart

Never can I think of to hurt

All my troubles they ease

When thee my eyes sees

When thy eyes tears

A thing that my heart fears

Ever with me I want thee to stay

A promise that I won't betray

All these feelings towards thee that I have

My heart says its because of love

Life is brief

My love don't stay engrossed somewhere and apart

Just open thy heart

And tell me how thee feel

Be it sadness or zeal

Very much in love with thee

When thee feel same don't forget to say it to me

Love, hug, cuddle, and kiss;

Often we need them and never should miss

Satisfy Thyself living thus,

That there should be no unfulfilled wish between us

Because when I cease to be

With regretful tears thee should not miss me

I wish our memories thee cherish

Now and even after I perish

Dear, time will pass by

Life is brief, soon a day will come to die

Fly me high

My love, I am your kite fly me high

Against the wind, up in the sky

At this high height

The world seems a beautiful sight

Nothing bothers much here

For your love for me is highest and pure

Only tranquillity surrounds

And to peace, my mind bonds

A greater purpose to my life

and in my life happiness is rife

There is contentment at heart

And disappointments apart

Finally from this place, above it, to rise

Thus to be liberated form desires by being wise

My love, I am your kite fly me high

Against the wind, up in the sky

My love, I am your kite fly me high

Against the wind, up in the sky

Glowing Lamp

What is oil to a lamp that is glowing

So is thy love to my life

I keeps me going

When darkness in rife

Disappointments when makes my eyes cloudy

It gives me a love that is steady

Amidst darkness it is the only one light

No matter what that shines bright

My beloved no matter what is my plight

I overcome it seeing glowing lamps light

I will be there

I will be there
In your leisure
And in moments of pleasure
In your every desire
Helping you to acquire
With you in your sorrow
For a better tomorrow
To share your trouble
And hold when tears dribble
Lightning a hope
In your despair to cope
When you get hurt
To make your broken heart
My love with you every time
Till the end of my time
I will be there
I will be there

It's all because of your love

It's all because of your love

Know my dear I live

You make my world seem beautiful

For I find your love dutiful

Owe you this happiness I carry

For you don't let me worry

You make me fly very high

For you make my burden less weigh

Love songs you make me sing

For I have a lovely being

At my heart I don't feel lone

For you don't let me alone

In every thing I find interest

For I am happy while I quest

It's all because of your love

Know my dear I live

It's all because of your love

Know my dear I live

Long way through

You make may life glow

With all the love you show

My love, the way you care

To find one like you is rare

We have been together

At all times, and stood apart never

Be it sunshine

Or darkest hours to remain

Together we did our daily chores

And our shopping outdoors

Be it our moments of joy, achievements, or vacations.

We were together in all occasions

Together we laughed

And together we cried

You are my moon and I am your light

Without you it will be a dark night

I can't think of life without you

For I have been loving you longway through.

Memories

The moments of intimacy that we share

Times of affection, oneness and care

Are heavenly memories that our souls bear

Which in this life will be always there

We wish to carry these fond memories after life

to be with us for time infinitely rife

Many feel like us

Many might have felt and many shall come to feel thus

But how pathetic it is dear

That memories lasts only till this life is there

Everything to end with death

No trace of them even if there be a rebirth

Lone wolf

Until I found you,, I was a lone wolf

My love, in no place I found comfort

With none to love, other than self

Led a renouncing life, for money fell short

A sweet pain my heart bore

Of an ideal imaginary love, in my solitude world

Someone I can adore

Having my real world remained lone and cold

I longed for a mate, who values less material desires

One who loves me apart from it

A soulmate, that my heart admirers

Who will always keep my world lit

Why Did We Fade Away

Why did we fade away, love?

Like whispers on the breeze,

The fire that once burned bright

Now flickers, ill at ease.

Did time, the thief of hearts, steal

The passion in your eyes?

Or has familiarity bred

A dullness in disguise?

The laughter, light and free,

Now echoes in the past.

The touch that sent shivers down

Is a memory built to last.

Where is the innocence,

The yearning in your gaze?

Replaced by a knowing look,

A web of practiced ways.

Only love binds us together,

With excitement to weather.

Let's fan the dying embers, love,

And bring our hearts together.

Lost paradise

It's still fresh in my mind
The days when we were to each other kind
Had love, compassion, and innocence
To each other's mistakes had tolerance
Those were the young days of our wed
We were happy even without butter in our bread
Somehow they got lost in virtuless ways
Leading us to joyless days
I wish we gather again all that is lost
Otherwise our happiness it will cost
Being happy not only benefits us dear
By being so, we also spread around cheer
We not only feel good when we have virtue
My soul mate, we spread goodness too
So dear don't think twice
We have to regain our lost paradise

Betrothal anniversary

I remember you walking with me side by side

Let I be happy or sad

Or be it my moment of disbelief

Or a moment of my grief Ever you were with me

Like my shadow to be

In my darkest hours of the night

You became my source of light

And ever kept me going

Your love towards me, a adivine one, in its being

I feel fortunate for this

For it is such a bliss

The more I saw of you

The more my love for you grew

Twenty four years way back you broke my solitude

Today is our betrothal anniversary,

A day to express my gratitude.

You never said "I love you"

Behind your anxious concern

There is a care hidden

Whenever for days we had to part

With a smile you hid your hurt

When i arrive late

For me you eagerly wait

Whenever I cried

You cried by my side

When I am in trouble

I see you tremble

You always did that for me

Which made me happy

You never said "I love you".

But your actions did its true

Beloved you know what

My heart feels even if you don't say that.

Go with your heart

Go with your heart

There is pain in going apart

Heart and mind both are distinct

Heart emotions and mind your intellect

Based on right and wrong functions mind

While heart purely on emotional ground

Right and wrong changes with time

But emotions, at all times, has the same theme

Sati Pratha, untouchable, Bal Vivah, once right

Emotion proved them wrong with lawful fight

Where the two hearts don't meet

And the relationship is not sweet

It's better for those hearts to keep distance

For they don't beat in oneness hence

About the Author

V.R. Venkateshan was born on 23/01/1968 in Pudukkottai, Tamil Nadu, his father Capt. V. Ramamurthy is from Vishnambattai, Tamil Nadu, and retired as chief pilot instructor from the Nagpur Flying Club. His Mother Mrs. Rajam Ramamurthy was a School Teacher. Venkateshan did his B.E. in Electronics and Power Engineering from Nagpur, Maharashtra. "Verse of wisdom " is an essence of what the author understood of life. The author believes that with knowledge many of our life's problems can be solved. The author strongly believes that his book can definitely transform people's lives.

Author's Message

Thank you for taking the time to read "verse of wisdom."

Your willingness to embark on this journey with me means the world to me, and I am deeply grateful for your presence.

I hope that the words on these pages have resonated with you in some way, and that they have provided you with moments of insight, comfort, and inspiration. Whether you have laughed, cried, or felt a sense of peace, my hope is that these poems have touched your heart in some way.

As you move forward on your own journey, remember that life is full of ups and downs, but it is the connections we make with one another that make it all worthwhile. Take the lessons you have learned here and apply them to your own life, and know that you are never alone.

Thank you again for being a part of this experience. May the beauty and power of poetry continue to enrich your life in countless ways.

9 798889 475480 2